WARRIORS
OF STONE

TITAN
COMICS

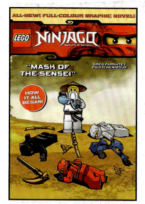

#6 WARRIORS OF STONE

GREG FARSHTEY • Writer

JOLYON YATES • Artist

JAYJAY JACKSON • Colourist

BRIAN SENKA • Letterer

PAULO HENRIQUE • Cover Artist

LAURIE E. SMITH • Cover Colourist

Titan
COMICS

LEGO® NINJAGO Masters of Spinjitzu
Volume Six: Warriors of Stone

Greg Farshtey – Writer
Joylon Yates – Artist
Jayjay Jackson – Colourist
Bryan Senka – Letterer

Published by Titan Comics, a division of Titan Publishing Group Ltd., 144 Southwark St., London, SE1 0UP. LEGO NINJAGO: VOLUME #6: WARRIORS OF STONE. LEGO, the LEGO logo and Ninjago are trademarks of the LEGO Group ©2014 The LEGO Group. All rights reserved. All characters, events and institutions depicted herein are fictional. Any similarity between any of the names, characters, persons, events and/or institutions in this publication to actual names, characters, and persons, whether living or dead and/or institutions are unintended and purely coincidental. License contact for Europe: Blue Ocean Entertainment AG, Germany.

A CIP catalogue record for this title is available from the British Library.

Printed in China.

First published in the USA and Canada in June 2013 by Papercutz.

10 9 8 7 6 5 4 3 2 1

ISBN: 9781782761976

www.titan-comics.com

www.LEGO.com

MEET THE MASTERS OF SPINJITZU...

JAY

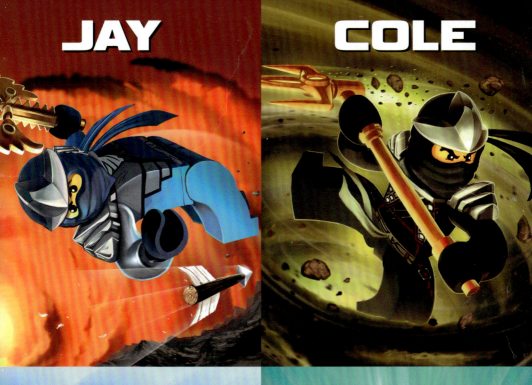

COLE

ZANE

KAI

And the Master of the Masters of Spinjitzu...

SENSEI WU

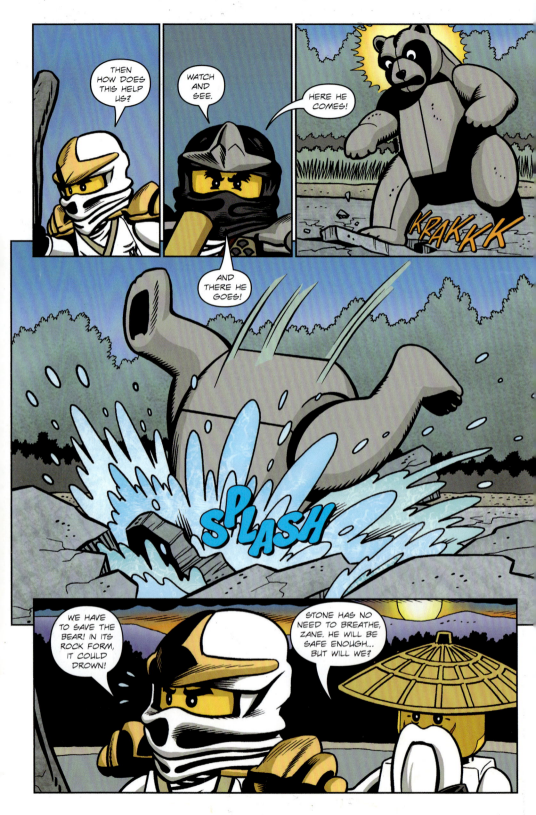

Others are about to learn the true meaning of fear...

I MUST CLEAR MY MIND OF ALL DISTRACTIONS AND BECOME IN TUNE WITH MY SUR-ROUNDINGS.

THESE PEOPLE HAVE CHANGED FORMS AND SEEM TO HAVE NO AWARENESS THAT THEY WERE EVER ANYTHING BUT STONE. WHY?

THEY HAVE FORGOTTEN THEIR PASTS... FORGOTTEN...

BURIED IT AWAY... SO DEEP IT CAN NEVER BE FOUND...

OH, NO! WHAT WE ARE SEEING IS ONLY THE BEGINNING-- AND IF WE DON'T FIND AN ANSWER SOON, NONE OF US WILL LEAVE THIS PLACE ALIVE!

OR PERHAPS IT IS ALREADY TOO LATE...?

Not far away, the Ninja have reunited to share what they have learned, which is--

NOTHING! WE'RE NO CLOSER TO FIGURING OUT WHAT'S GOING ON HERE.

IT TURNED TO ROCK! WHAT AM I SUPPOSED TO DO WITH A STONE SHURIKEN AGAINST STONE PEOPLE?

YOU'RE WRONG, KAI, WE KNOW SOME THINGS NOW...

WE KNOW THAT NO ONE REMEMBERS THEIR LIVES BEFORE THEY TURNED TO STONE...

OR EVEN THAT ANYTHING STRANGE HAS HAPPENED TO THEM.

I SAW SOMETHING MOST *DISTURBING*, COLE.

MORE DISTURBING THAN A ROCK SHURIKEN?

"I OBSERVED A VILLAGER, AN ARTIST, SPENDING HOURS SCULPTING THE FIGURE OF A BIRD," ZANE REVEALS.

"THEN HE TURNED AND ACCIDENTALLY SMASHED HIS WORK OF ART."

KRASH

"AND HE DID NOT CARE," FINISHES ZANE. "HOURS, PROBABLY WEEKS OF WORK, AND ITS RUIN MEANT **NOTHING** TO HIM."

MAYBE HE JUST DIDN'T LIKE HOW IT CAME OUT.

NO, JAY. I THINK IT IS SOMETHING MORE **SINISTER**. I THINK AS THEIR BODIES TURN TO STONE, SO TOO DO THEIR HEARTS.

THEY STOP CARING. SO WE NOT ONLY HAVE TO SAVE THEM FROM THIS TRANSFORMATION, BUT SAVE THEM FROM THEMSELVES.

AND WE BETTER DO IT SOON-- I CAN FEEL MY RIGHT LEG TURNING TO ROCK. PRETTY SOON, WE'LL ALL TRANSFORM.

UNFORTUNATELY, YOU WON'T BE THAT LUCKY, NINJA. **YOU'RE ALL UNDER ARREST!**

AGAIN? WHY IS IT EVERY TIME WE GO TO A CITY, SOMEONE TRIES TO THROW US IN JAIL?

MUST BE YOUR CHARM, JAY.

WE CAN'T AFFORD TO BE STOPPED. **TAKE THEM, TEAM!**

YOU WERE THE GREATEST THREAT TO MY PLANS, SENSEI -- BUT NOW YOU'RE THINKING DIFFERENTLY, AREN'T YOU?
STONE IS HARD. STONE MUST RULE. ALL WHO ARE SOFT AND WEAK WILL BE CRUSHED BENEATH OUR FEET!

33

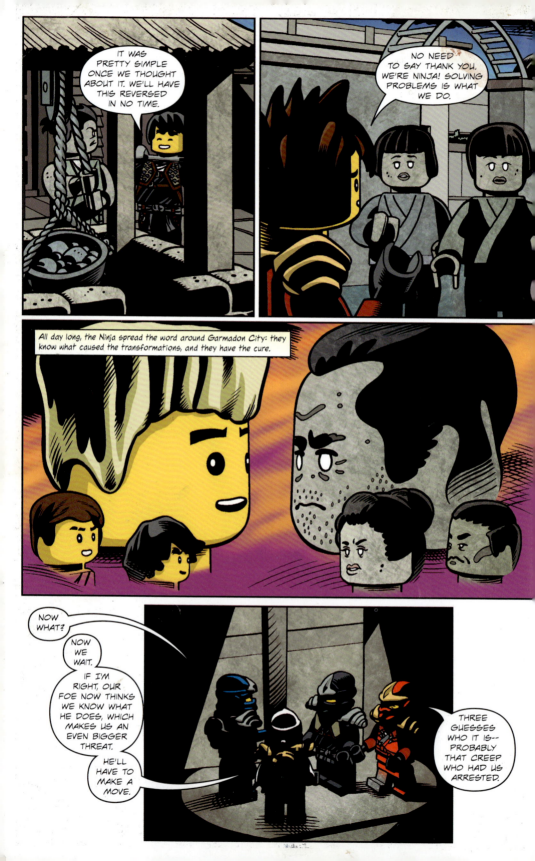

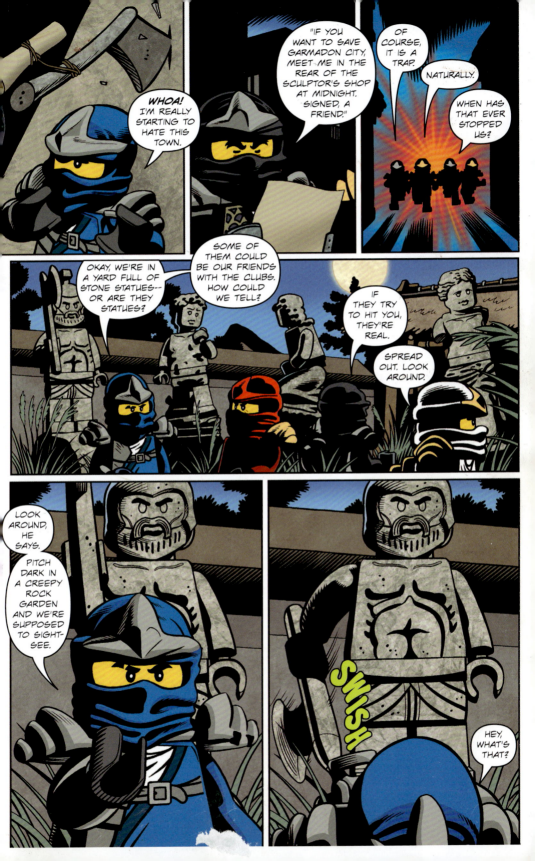

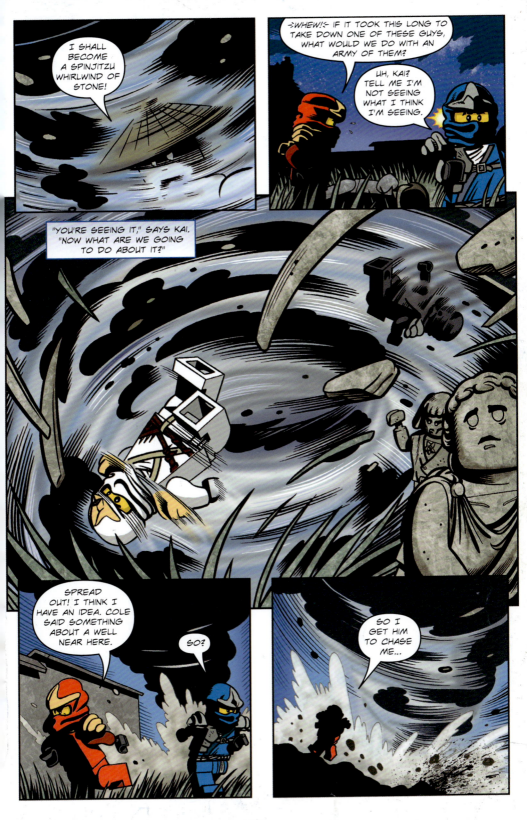

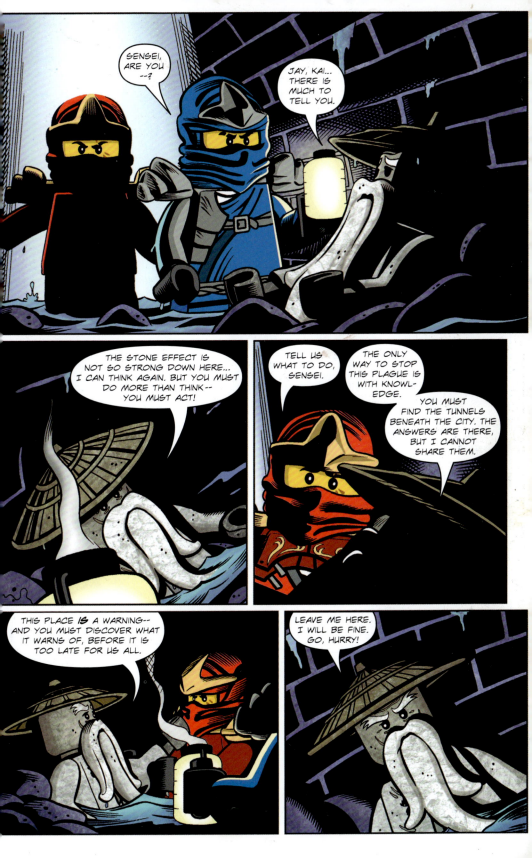

47

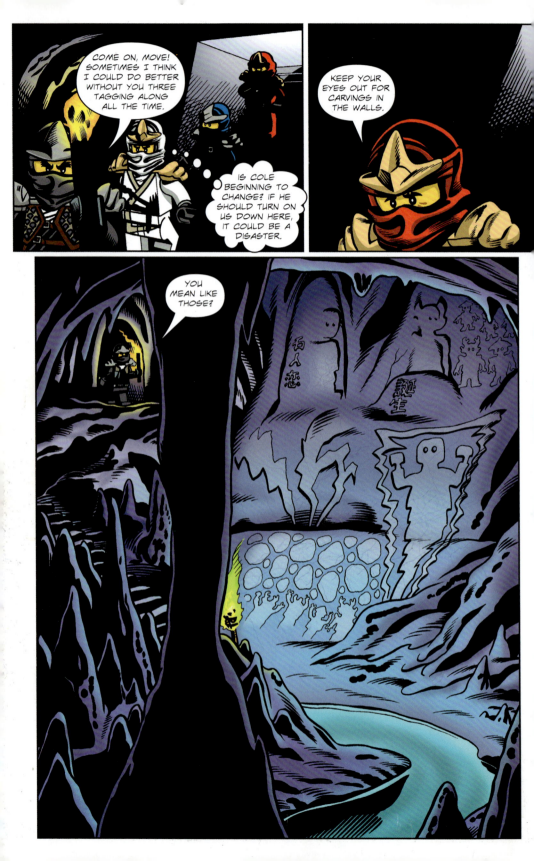

"ACCORDING TO THIS," SAYS ZANE, "FOUR BRAVE NINJA WILL CHALLENGE THE MIGHT OF THE STONE WARRIORS-- AND BE UTTERLY DEFEATED!"

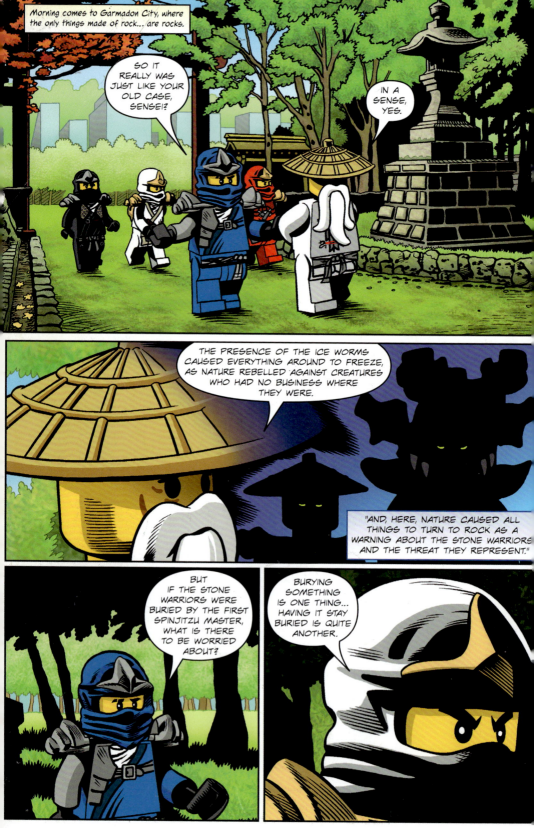

THEN THE STONE WARRIORS COULD BE LOOSE EVEN NOW...

THEY COULD MAKE FIGHTING SKELETONS AND SNAKES LOOK LIKE A TEA PARTY.

INDEED.

MY FATHER NEVER SPOKE OF THEM, EXCEPT TO SAY THAT NINJAGO HAD BEEN SPARED A TERRIBLE FATE.

SO WHAT DO WE DO?

WHAT WE ALWAYS DO, POWERS OR NO POWERS: WE TRAIN, WE PREPARE, WE MAKE SURE WE'RE READY FOR WHATEVER HAPPENS.

RIGHT. WHAT HE SAID.

OF COURSE, COLE IS RIGHT.

BUT ONE THING BOTHERS ME-- IF WE CAME SO CLOSE TO DEFEAT FIGHTING FARMERS, BAKERS, AND ARTISTS TURNED TO ROCK...

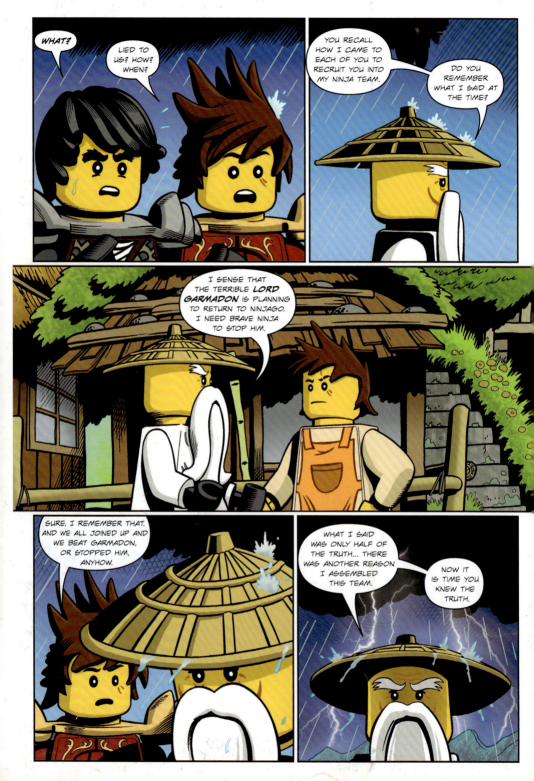

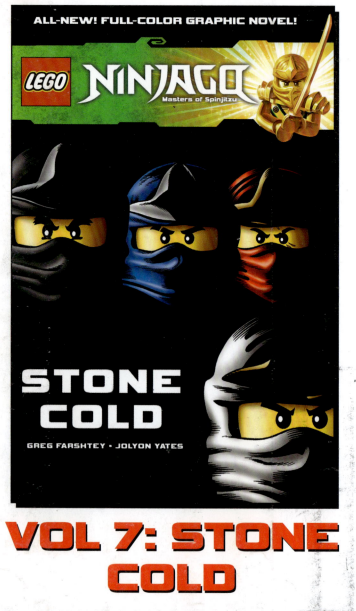